GIVE THANKS

Notice the good stuff!

Naomi Shulman
illustrated by Hsinping Pan

Storey Publishing

For my father, Alvin, and my husband, Jonathan.
I Am Thankful
for both of them each and every day.

The mission of Storey Publishing is to serve our customers by publishing practical information that encourages personal independence in harmony with the environment.

Edited by Deanna F. Cook and Sarah Guare
Art direction and book design by Carolyn Eckert
Text production by Slavica A. Walzl
Illustrations by © Hsinping Pan

Text © 2021 by Naomi Shulman

Storey Publishing
210 MASS MoCA Way
North Adams, MA 01247
storey.com

Printed in China through World Print
10 9 8 7 6 5 4 3 2 1

978-1-63586-399-4

0722/B1890/A8

Todah!

Two of the first words you learned when you were little were "thank you" (*todah* in Hebrew). Saying thank you to people is polite, but it's also much more. There's a famous saying in *Pirkei Avot* (*Ethics of the Ancestors*, an ancient collection of Jewish wisdom): "Who is rich? Those who are happy with what they have." But first we have to tune in to all the goodness that surrounds us.

That's where the Jewish value of *hakarat hatov* (Hebrew for "noticing the good") comes in. It's easy! Start by looking around for good things—a friend smiling, a cat purring, a kind word someone said to you. All of us have things we can be grateful for. The games and activities in this book will help you take a moment to stop and notice them.

Feeling grateful makes us happier. Expressing thanks to others can help them feel happier, too. In Judaism, finding ways to do this is a *mitzvah* ("commandment" or good deed)— even if it's as simple as playing "I Spy" or baking a cupcake.

So turn the page and get ready to say *todah*!

Boker Tov!
Good Morning!

When you wake up, think about how amazing it is to start a new day. Anything can happen. What are you looking forward to in the next hour? **What are you excited about today?**

When you first open your eyes,
there's a special Hebrew blessing
you can say: Modeh Ani,
which means "I am grateful."

Modeh ani l'fanecha,
melech chai v'kayam,
shehechezarta bi nishmati,
b'chemla raba emunatecha.

Play Mirror Mirror

Nice teeth!

When you brush your teeth, look in the mirror and
**tell yourself one thing
you like about yourself.**
There's nothing like having a friendly face
remind you of all the great things
you have going for you!

Look Out Your Window

How many good things can you count?

Play
I Spy Gratitude

On your way to school,
notice things you see and say
what is special about them.

I spy ... **a bird!**
She makes
beautiful music.

Make
Gratitude
Graffiti!

Using washable chalk, leave a message on the sidewalk about something you are thankful for.

Other people will see it
and may think about what they are
grateful for, too.

Hold a
Thank-You
Sale

of items you no longer need.

SALE

When you sell something,
tell the buyer why you loved it.
It's more fun when
lots of households do this together.

You can raise money for tzedakah ("justice" or charity).

Giving tzedakah helps make the world better—
and that is something we can all feel thankful for.

Thank Your Community!

What are some of your favorite spots near where you live?

Thank the folks who make these places special.

Bake Grateful Cupcakes!

Use a frosting pen to write a grateful message like *todah rabah* (Hebrew for "thank you very much").

Conduct a
Thank-You
Chorus

You know who
deserves a note of applause?
Your teacher!

During recess, gather some of your classmates to practice a (short!) song.

Sing the song to your teacher when you go back into the classroom.

Plant Seeds of Thankfulness!

In the spring, gather a few paper cups,
some flower seeds, and some potting soil.
As you put each seed in the dirt,
think about something you are grateful for.

Each time you water your seeds,
think about those things.

Watch your seeds
flower and
your gratitude grow!

SEED

Hug a Tree

Trees give
so much—
shade, fruits
and nuts,
homes for
animals, and
clean air.

Put your hands on its trunk.
Tell it thanks
for being so strong!

Learn to Say
Thank You in Different Languages
Make everybody feel good!

TODAH
(Hebrew)

XIE XIE
(Mandarin)

GRACIAS
(Spanish)

MERCI
(French)

SHUKRAN
(Arabic)

ARIGATO
(Japanese)

ASANTE
(Swahili)

Thank you!
(American Sign Language)

1. Put your fingers on your mouth. Your hand should be flat.

2. Move your hand down and toward the person you are thanking.

3. Smile (so they'll know you mean it).

Have a
Family Hug
Hug the people you love
for no reason at all
except that you're grateful for them.

Appreciate the Animals!

The mitzvah of *tza'ar ba'alei chayim*,
or caring for animals, helps remind us that all critters—
even the buzzing, biting insects—
play a role in our ecosystem.

**Thank a bee
for pollinating
a flower!**

**Gently move a worm
from a hot sidewalk
to the cool grass.**
It will feel more comfortable.

Todah!

Be a Helper

Even doing small
things around the house
is part of *tikkun olam*,
or repairing the world.

Carry your dirty dishes
to the sink.

Sweep up
and make the room tidy.

Empty the trash
so the room smells good.

Show your pets you're grateful by taking care of them.

Brush your cat, walk the dog, or scrub out the fish bowl.

Keep a
Gratitude Journal

When you write down what you're thankful for,
it makes you happy! Grab a notebook or staple
together some blank sheets of paper. You can . . .

Write one word a day
that sums up what you're feeling grateful for.

Every Friday, write or draw about
**the best thing that happened
in the last week.**
Who was there? What did you do?
How did you feel?

Notice the Good Stuff!

(Hakarat hatov is what it's all about!)

**Feeling sad or worried?
Ask yourself these questions
and watch your mood
turn around in no time!**

What is my **first happy memory**?

What is **something fun** that I did this week?

What is my **favorite thing**
about my neighborhood?

What animals did I see today?

What **wonderful smells** did I notice today?

What **free things** am I thankful for?

What is **something interesting** that I heard today?

Who **makes me laugh** the hardest?

Make a Special
Thank-You Picture!

Draw a picture of a gift you received.

Send the picture as a thank-you to the person who gave you the gift.

When the person who gave you a gift
can't be there to see you open it,
snap a photo or take a video
of you opening the gift!

**Then send the
photo or video**
to the person who
sent the gift.

Build a Happiness Wall

At the end of each day, think of something wonderful that happened.

Write or draw it on a sticky note,
then hang it up!

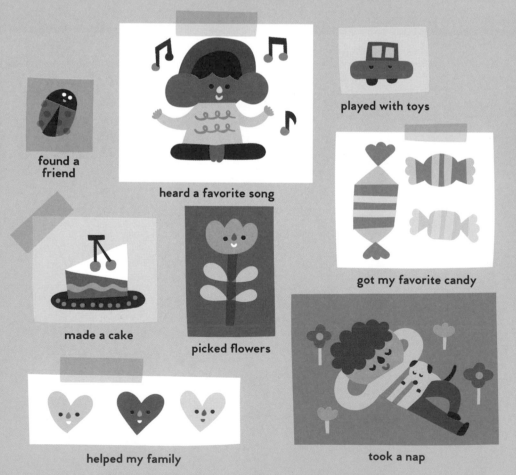

found a friend

heard a favorite song

played with toys

made a cake

picked flowers

got my favorite candy

helped my family

took a nap

saw my grandparents

played with my cat

saw a rainbow

felt the sunshine

got a gift

sat next to a friend at lunch

saw a cool bug

ate ice cream

watered a plant

Over time, watch the wall fill with wonderful things that you feel thankful for.

Put Gratitude on the Menu!

Go around the table and ask
each person to say
one thing they're thankful for.

(Don't forget to thank the person
who put dinner on the table!)

Many families say a blessing before they eat.

What's the most delicious thing you ate today?

What feels good right now?

What happened today that you're proud of?

Who did something nice for you today?

Play the
Alphabet
Gratitude Game

**One person begins by naming
something they're grateful for
that starts with the letter A.**

The next person chooses something that starts
with the letter B, and so on until you get to the letter Z.

E
Elephants

B
Butterflies

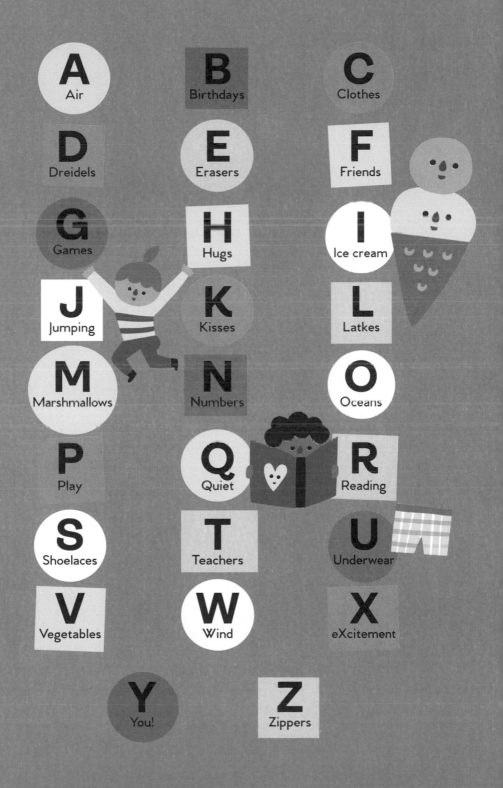

A Air

B Birthdays

C Clothes

D Dreidels

E Erasers

F Friends

G Games

H Hugs

I Ice cream

J Jumping

K Kisses

L Latkes

M Marshmallows

N Numbers

O Oceans

P Play

Q Quiet

R Reading

S Shoelaces

T Teachers

U Underwear

V Vegetables

W Wind

X eXcitement

Y You!

Z Zippers

Go on a Gratitude
Scavenger Hunt

The next time you go for a walk, look for something that:

smells good

looks cute

feels warm

feels cool

makes you laugh

is tasty

is your favorite color

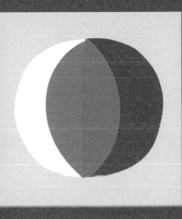

is fun to play with

Picture Challenge:

Take a photo—or draw a picture!—
of all the things you found.

Play
Thank-You Hopscotch

Draw a hopscotch grid on the ground.

In each square, instead of numbers, write types of things you are thankful for, like "friends," "food," and "toys."

toys

colors

clothes

For each theme square you land on, **name a thing or person you love.**

DUMPLINGS

sports

nature

food

music

animals

friends

family

Appreciate Sick Days

Feeling icky is no fun,
but are there any good parts?

Maybe you are cozy in bed
with hot matzo ball soup and soft tissues.
Look for the good things and
you might start to feel better faster.

Carry a Thankful Stone

Find a small, smooth rock and put it in your pocket.
Every time you touch the stone,
think of something you are thankful for.

Give a Flower to a Friend

Cut petals out of paper.

On each petal, write something
about your friend that makes you smile.
Glue the petals together.
Give the flower to your friend
to show how much you like them.

The more grateful you are,
the more good feelings bloom.

Take a Deep Breath

Breathe in through your nose
and say a silent thank-you to yourself.

Breathe out through your mouth and
**say a silent thank-you to
someone else.**
Now notice how calm you feel.

At bedtime, do a

Gratitude Countdown!

Think of three things from the day that you are thankful for.

What happened today that made you smile?

Who did something nice for you?

What memories did you make?

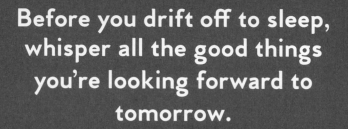

Before you drift off to sleep,
whisper all the good things
you're looking forward to
tomorrow.